Christma

To my God-son
Wishing you a very happy
Christmas with lots
of love
from
"G-M" Wendy xxxx

THE BOY, A KITCHEN, AND HIS CAVE

THE TALE OF ST EUPHROSYNOS THE COOK

CATHERINE K. CONTOPOULOS

Illustrated by
Chrissanth Greene-Gross

ST VLADIMIR'S SEMINARY PRESS • CRESTWOOD, NEW YORK • 2002

AUTHOR DEDICATION:
To my beloved Lily who inspires me every day.

ILLUSTRATOR DEDICATION:
For Natasha, Nicholas, and Daria, Slava Bogu.

The publication of this book was made possible through a gift made in memory of Mrs Sophie Koulomzin (†2000), author, teacher, and pioneer in Orthodox Christian education.

LIBRARY OF CONGRESS CATALOGING-IN-PUBLICATION DATA

Contopoulos, Catherine K.
    The boy, a kitchen, and his cave : the tale of St. Euphrosynos the cook / Catherine K. Contopoulos; illustrated by Chrissanth Greene-Gross.
        p. cm.
     Summary: Relates the legend of Euphrosynos, an uncultured peasant boy who became a cook in a Greek monastery at an early age, and whose humility and joy in God's creation led him to be named a saint.
    ISBN 0-88141-241-4
    1. Euphrosynos, the Cook, Saint, 9th cent—Juvenile literature.
    2. Christian saints—Greece—Biography—Juvenile literature.
    [1. Euphrosynos, the Cook, Saint, 9th cent. 2. Saints.] I. Greene-Gross, Chrissanth, ill. II. Title.

BX619.E95 C66 2002
270.3'092—DC21   2002068113

ST VLADIMIR'S SEMINARY PRESS
575 Scarsdale Road • Crestwood • New York • 10707-1699
1-800-204-BOOK

ISBN 0-88141-241-4

Book and cover design: Amber Schley Houx

PRINTED IN HONG KONG

Tucked away in the mountains of northern Greece was a remote and tiny village of farmers and shepherds where there lived a young boy named Euphrosynos. His family was very poor and needed Euphrosynos and his older brother to work on their farm. Once they became old enough, the boys stopped going to school, and instead they shepherded sheep and goats, gathered olives from the trees, and planted tomatoes, eggplants, bell peppers, and green beans. Euphrosynos liked to help his mother bake bread.

Euphrosynos did not mind not being able to go to school. He never found it easy to concentrate on his studies or understand what little he could read. And the other children teased him for always lagging behind and being unable to finish his homework. His brother patiently tutored him every evening, and Euphrosynos was grateful to him, but he still found it difficult to keep up.

Euphrosynos' mother and father took the family to church every Sunday. Euphrosynos loved the hymns of the services, and over time he learned the words and the melodies and sang along with everyone else. And he sang while he worked in the fields. He could feel God was with him, watching over him while he worked long hours in the hot sun or in the cold rain and mud. These things he understood with his whole heart, and he was happy.

One afternoon Euphrosynos' father sent him into town to buy cheese as a special treat for dinner that evening. This was the first time that his father had given Euphrosynos the opportunity to run an errand in town. Usually his brother went, but today he was cleaning out the storage barrels for the olives and could not go. Euphrosynos was very excited about the prospect of doing something for his father in town on his own.

"A pound of graviera, Euphrosynos," said his father, as he gave the boy enough coins to pay for the cheese.

"Yes, Father, I know the one. It's my favorite," said Euphrosynos.

At the cheese store in the village, Euphrosynos approached the counter. The cheese monger bellowed in a loud voice, "Yes, boy? What will you take today?"

All the cheeses in the store, however, dazzled Euphrosynos. He had never seen such a variety of shapes, sizes, colors, and smells!

"Cheese, please, sir," was all Euphrosynos could muster, as he put his coins on the counter.

"That is what we have here indeed—cheese! But what kind of cheese would you like, boy?" asked the cheese monger, who was beginning to lose his patience.

Euphrosynos heard more customers filling the store, waiting in a line behind him to buy their cheese and yogurt. But Euphrosynos realized he had forgotten the name of his favorite cheese! He looked at all the cheeses on display, hoping to recognize the one he came to buy, but he could not. He felt more confused than ever. All the cheeses began to look the same. There were so many!

"Well, boy? Is this some sort of joke?" thundered the cheese monger.

"What's the problem?" shouted an irritated customer in line behind Euphrosynos.

"Are you buying cheese or aren't you?" griped another.

"What an idiot! He's just standing there!" complained another.

Euphrosynos felt a cold panic take hold of him. He could not speak. His body froze where he stood. He felt his face redden in embarrassment.

"Foolish boy! Get out of my store!" yelled the cheese monger.

Euphrosynos
heard cackles
of laughter
all around him.
Some of the
other children of
the village had gathered
around, and they were laughing at him
too. Euphrosynos ran out of the store and felt tiny
stones shower his back. With the villagers' jeers bursting in his ears,
he ran all the way home. Tears tumbled down his cheeks as he told his father
what had happened.

"It's all my fault, Father. I forgot the name of the cheese! And then I felt so ashamed! I am so stupid…
so very stupid…" Euphrosynos said, shaking his head in misery.

"You're not stupid, my son," his father said, taking his small hand in his big one. "God has given each of
us different strengths and weaknesses. You must not be afraid of the world, Euphrosynos. We must all live on
God's earth together. For this reason he has made each of us different. Your strengths lie elsewhere,
in your pure heart."

Euphrosynos hugged his father, but the pain he felt did not go away.

When he grew up, Euphrosynos' brother decided to marry. His father gave him half the family farm as a wedding gift. "It is all I have to give you, my son. And you greatly deserve it."

Euphrosynos insisted that his brother be given his share as well.

"But why?" asked his father. "One day you too will marry and have your own family, and you must have a farm of your own as well."

"Father," said Euphrosynos, "I thank you for this great gift you wish to give me, but I do not want to manage my own property. My brother has good ideas to improve the farm. He will be a great success. I am not a clever man and have no such desires, and it would pain me to deprive my brother of all that he could have. As for me, I would like to live a simpler life somewhere else. And I know God will help me to find it."

His brother thanked him for his great gift. After his brother married and took over the farm, Euphrosynos felt it was the right time for him to strike out on his own. With tears in her eyes and a brave smile on her lips, his mother said to him, "You are my delight, my dearest son, and that is why I named you *Euphrosynos*, which means 'cheery' or 'merry'. Now it is time for you to find your own happiness, wherever that may be." His mother gave him a small icon of the *Theotokos*, the Virgin Mary, to keep him safe and remind him of her love. He said his good-byes to his beloved family and left.

Euphrosynos prayed for the Lord to lead him along the right way as he followed different paths through the valleys and the mountains. He met many people who hired him to work on their farms, and they gave him food to eat and a place to sleep at night.

One very hot afternoon, tired after a difficult walk, he was relieved to see a village up ahead. He stopped at the fountain in the square for a rest and a drink of water. Euphrosynos sat on the stone pavement and whispered a prayer of thanks to the Lord for the village and the cool, refreshing water of the fountain. Three men dressed in brightly colored robes were gathered around the fountain as well. Euphrosynos overheard them talking excitedly about a special place from which they had just returned.

"How uplifting it was!"

"How at peace I feel!"

"I'm a different person, truly I am!"

"Excuse me, good sirs," said Euphrosynos as politely as he knew how, "may I ask how I can get to this place?"

"Dear boy, we are talking about the monasteries of Mount Athos. We have just spent many weeks there as pilgrims."

"Pilgrims?"

"Those who seek to be closer to God and his peace, away from the busy, everyday world," replied one of the gentlemen pilgrims.

"Tell me, please, where this place is, so that I too may be closer to God and his peace," begged Euphrosynos.

The pilgrims drew Euphrosynos a map in the sand and went over the directions with him many times to make sure he understood where to go. They gave him a small loaf of bread to keep him strong on his journey. Euphrosynos thanked the kind pilgrims and set off.

Euphrosynos found Mount Athos three days later. In this one region there were many monasteries. No villages, no busy towns, only houses of the Lord where men lived and worked together, each dedicating his life to God. Euphrosynos felt a bubble of joy rise in his heart. He knew this was where God meant him to be.

Euphrosynos visited several monasteries. He saw how the monks painted beautiful icons on wood to decorate churches and on paper to illustrate marvelous holy books. He saw others reading from holy manuscripts and taking notes. Euphrosynos was filled with great admiration for these sacred talents the monks possessed, but he also felt anxious, for he had none of these skills. Would a monastery accept him even though he was not clever?

One day he visited a monastery where he saw workers threshing wheat in the fields. He joined in and helped with the harvesting. He sang as he worked, and the other monks smiled at him and sang with him. Once the sun began to set and the work was finished, he said a prayer of thanks to the Lord for his day and the beautiful wheat fields of the monastery, and with his right hand he made the sign of the cross on his chest.

not very smart and not worthy to be here, but if I could be of service in the fields or at some other job, perhaps I could stay with you?"

"My son, we are all meant to serve. I am the Abbot of this monastery, its spiritual leader, and yet I do my part and work for the good of our monastery in any way I can."

Euphrosynos was very surprised. This considerate, gentle man who worked by his side all day long was the leader of the monastery!

"But to work out here in the fields all day long, Your Grace?" asked Euphrosynos with respect. "Such work is not for a great leader, a man touched by the Holy Spirit such as you, but for someone like me, who is meant for hard labor."

"In the eyes of the Lord, my son, each of us is special and each one of us is equal. Only we make the differences between ourselves an obstacle. You are welcome to stay with us. Although we do not need more workers for our small farm, we do need a cook for our kitchen. Our cook is old and much too tired for such work. Would you cook for us?"

One monk approached him and asked him to return to the monastery with the others for dinner.

"You are a hard worker, my son," said the monk.

"The Lord helps me in all that I do, Father. I ask his blessing as I work and thank him when I am done. And I know he is with me. He brought me here to help you with your fields today, did he not?"

"Yes, my son, and you have been a great help," agreed the monk.

"I would like to keep helping, Father. I am no scholar,

mastered, with every pan, baking dish, and mixing spoon he scrubbed, with every apple and pear and potato he peeled, and with every carrot he chopped, Euphrosynos sang the hymns he had sung in the fields. Although he missed working outside in the fresh air and sun, Euphrosynos realized the great importance of cooking. With God's blessing and guidance, he was helping to transform the bounty of the Lord's earth into wholesome nourishment for the monks. As he picked carrots from the garden for the evening's soup, he admired their deep, orange color. He took a cracking bite of a carrot and was surprised by its rich sweetness.

"That is a good carrot, Lord!" he exclaimed heavenward. Euphrosynos felt the pilgrims' peace. He had found a place where he belonged.

Euphrosynos was thrilled. He immediately accepted the offer and went back to the monastery for dinner with the kind Abbot. There the Abbot introduced him to the old cook, and Euphrosynos began helping him right away by cleaning up the dishes.

"I am glad you are here, Euphrosynos," said the old cook. "My hands ache with pains, and I can no longer use them to work."

"Now you will rest, Cook," said Euphrosynos.

Euphrosynos eagerly attended to his duties. He cleaned all the vegetables and prepared them, just as Cook told him. Cook showed him how to make stewed okra, bean soups, grilled fish, rice pilaf, boiled dandelion greens, and tomato salads. With every new recipe Euphrosynos

Each day after lunch Euphrosynos had several hours to spend as he wished before he needed to begin to prepare dinner. He explored the grounds of the monastery, which was built on a cliff overlooking the sea. He enjoyed watching the foamy, white waves cap the rich, blue water. He had never spent time by the sea before and found it thrilling. He made the sign of the cross and thanked God for the shimmering sea and the salty wind blustering above.

One day as he was hiking by the sea, he found a cave hidden in the rocky cliffs. From inside he could hear the seawaters booming and crashing along the rocks below and the winds howling on the cliffs. Euphrosynos closed his eyes and delighted in nature's music. He decided this would be his special place, his sanctuary. He took the icon his mother had given him out of his pocket and perched it on a tiny shelf he had made out of pebbles. He sang his favorite hymn and smiled.

Euphrosynos walked to his cave every afternoon. There he sat quite still, listening to the raw delights of the sea beyond the cliffs, the battling winds, the seagulls swooping down, and the distant bells of the chapel. His heart was full, and he savored the presence of the Holy Spirit in all these things.

One evening after cleaning the dinner dishes, Euphrosynos was scrubbing the kitchen floor with a big, bristly brush and lots of soapy water in an old, tin bucket. He did not notice that the soapy water had begun to stream out of the kitchen and into the hallway. All of a sudden Euphrosynos heard a loud *Thwack! Thump! Boom!* One of the brother monks had slipped in the water and fallen! And the papers he had been holding were floating through the air!

"Oh no!" cried Euphrosynos.

"You foolish boy!" cried the monk. "I am rushing to get to a very important assembly, and your sloppiness has caused me to be late! My papers!! They're ruined! Oh, my backside! You foolish—fool!!"

"I beg your forgiveness, holy Father," Euphrosynos said ashamedly, "You are most right. I have used too much water and soap to clean my kitchen, and my ignorance caused this flood. Now I know not to use so much water and soap. I am so sorry to have caused you this accident. Today the Lord has shown me I need to be more careful in my work."

Euphrosynos helped the monk to his feet and offered him a towel with which to dry his black robes. The brother collected his wet papers and scowled at Euphrosynos one last time before he hurried down the hallway to the great hall.

Euphrosynos noticed the other monks rushing to the great hall to attend the weekly assembly. He put away his tin bucket and his brush, dried his hands and knees, and ran to the service entrance of the great hall through the dining room. He was so very curious to hear one of their discussions. Oh, the things he would learn tonight!

Euphrosynos stood in the shadows of the secret doorway at the back of the room.

"We are here to discuss the Kingdom of Heaven!" announced the Abbot. A murmur of excitement rippled through the room.

Euphrosynos listened carefully to the debate and tried to follow their discussion. But he could not understand the big words the wise monks were using or their quick, clever reasoning. The Abbot was leading the discussion and would often nod his head. Other times, he would raise his hand to stop a disagreement or to offer his opinion. At times, the discussion would make the brothers tremble with excitement or grumble with annoyance. No one, however, could agree on anything, and so the Abbot was disappointed. Everyone had so many different theories and ideas, but what was the Truth of God?

Euphrosynos retreated into the dark passageway, and a tear fell from his eye. He felt stupid. He could not understand what the monks were saying. He ran to his cave, where he always felt happy and at ease. Once there, he breathed in the fresh sea air, closed his eyes, and sitting quite still, listened to the soothing sounds the Lord's earth brought him, and he was thankful.

That evening the Abbot went to sleep and dreamt he was in a beautiful, lush garden, a true paradise. He saw a man standing by an apple tree, and on closer look, the Abbot was greatly surprised to see it was Euphrosynos, the cook!

Euphrosynos said to him, "I am looking upon the Kingdom of Heaven, the wondrous works of our Lord, and it is beautiful!" He cut a branch from the apple tree and gave it to the Abbot. But before the Abbot could thank him, Euphrosynos had turned away. As the Abbot called to him, the dream ended, and he awoke with a jolt. He sat up in his cot and realized his hands were clutching an apple tree branch with three rosy apples hanging from it, just like the one Euphrosynos had given him in the dream!

"Oh, this was no ordinary dream…" thought the Abbot.

That dawn at matins, the Abbot brought the apple branch with him and excitedly described his vision of Euphrosynos to the other monks.

"Dear brothers, I prayed last night for answers following our great discussion. And the Lord has answered my prayers."

"What could that peasant boy possibly teach us?" said one monk, with some indignation.

"Brother, that simple peasant boy who cooks our meals and cleans our kitchen lives his life in the true spirit of Christ. He is content with all that is before him. He sees plenty in everything, even when he has nothing. He appreciates all the small things of his day—how well his spoon ladles our soup, the sweetness of a carrot. And he praises the Lord at every turn!"

"Yes, it's true," said the monk who had slipped on Euphrosynos' soapy water. "Even when he spilled water from his bucket and made a mess, he thanked God for teaching him a new lesson. I was so annoyed with his carelessness, yet he was able to transform the mishap into a gift from above."

"You see, brothers," said the Abbot. "Our cook asks for nothing more than what is given to him. Everything in his life, each new day, is a chance to participate in the Kingdom of Heaven. Is this not what Jesus meant—that God's Kingdom is in our midst on earth?"

"I am convinced," continued the Abbot, "that God has blessed us by bringing Euphrosynos here to us. It is we who must learn from Euphrosynos, brothers! God's love knows no distinction of rank. Who are we to decide what or who is holy in God's eyes? Are we not all worthy of his grace? The apple branch is a sacred sign of the boy's place in the eyes of God. Euphrosynos' virtues run deep—his kindness and mildness, his modesty, his pure way of thinking. Yes, he is simple, but he is honest and full of love. Is this not what God intended for us? And are we so full of ourselves that we cannot see it?"

The monks scratched their heads and tugged on their beards as they considered all that the Abbot had said. And one by one they each agreed that the dream was a sign from God. They each kissed the apple branch in respect and sang a hymn of thanks to the Lord for Euphrosynos.

Later that morning, when Euphrosynos served the monks their breakfast of dark bread and berries, he noticed that they were all staring at him in a strange way. Euphrosynos grew uncomfortable and hurried back to the kitchen. The Abbot followed him inside. In the corner of the kitchen the old cook was sitting in his favorite chair, sipping chamomile tea.

The Abbot told Euphrosynos about his vision. "God has favored you with his grace, dear boy. This is a great gift, a great honor!"

"But the apples?" asked Euphrosynos, as he watched the monk carefully lay them on the counter. "I do not understand these things. They frighten me."

"Do not be afraid, my son. In the dream I saw you in a beautiful garden, much like Paradise where Adam and Eve once lived."

"But Father, they fell from grace when they ate the apple from the tree," said Euphrosynos.

"Yes, but by your example you show us how we can return to that harmony with God!"

"My hands, my hands!" the old cook cried as he trembled, sinking to his knees. One of the apples lay on the counter, a bite having been taken out of it.

"I ate from one of the apples and now my hands are supple once more! This is a miracle! A miracle!" he sputtered, as he excitedly made the sign of the cross. "That is truly a holy apple!"

The other monks heard the commotion in the kitchen and came running to see. The old cook showed them his healed hands, no longer curled and withered with pain, but strong and nimble.

"A miracle! A miracle!" they all cried with great joy.

Soon many, many people, having heard of the healing powers of Euphrosynos' apples, came to visit the monastery to be blessed and healed. But all this attention made Euphrosynos uneasy. He could no longer find time alone to go to his cave and listen to God's music, nor could he continue to cook and clean the way he used to.

"You can no longer cook and clean for us, Euphrosynos!" the monks told him. "You are a holy man. Such work is beneath you now!"

But Euphrosynos did not agree and told the Abbot so.

"Your Grace, I do not deserve all this attention. I am not a special, powerful person. All these people who come to the monastery are looking to me for comfort and miracles, but these things are from God, not from me. I cannot be what these people want me to be. I am no teacher, no celebrity. I simply wish to work quietly, to serve," he said.

Euphrosynos asked the Abbot for permission to leave the monastery.

"I know you have given this much thought and prayed for guidance, my son," said the Abbot. "I give you permission to leave. You must follow your heart's desire.

And God will lead you to it. Your presence here has changed us all forever. Go, my son, and God grant you many years."

The Abbot and Euphrosynos hugged each other farewell. Euphrosynos packed his knapsack with his few belongings and left the monastery. He passed by his cave one last time. He decided to leave his icon of the *Theotokos* there as an offering of thanks.

"It is all I have to give, dear Lord," said Euphrosynos. "Perhaps someone else one day will find this beautiful cave as I did, and find great joy in it, being with you and your wonderful music. For I know now that I will carry that music in my heart wherever I go."

Euphrosynos kissed the icon good-bye. He left the cave, and taking the rocky path along the cliffs above the sea, sang his favorite hymn as he walked.

FOR YEARS AND YEARS the
legend of the young cook and his
pure spirit spread throughout
the countryside, and many
pilgrims came to honor
the monastery where he
had lived and worked
so faithfully. Many
looked for
Euphrosynos,
but never
found him.
The kind, old
Abbot knew
that wherever
Euphrosynos was,
deep in his heart,
he was the happiest
of men.

To the right is an icon of Saint Euphrosynos the Cook as he is remembered in the tradition of the Orthodox Church.

The feast day of Saint Euphrosynos is celebrated on September 11th. The troparion here is the hymn sung during church services on that day.

Ὁ ἅγιος   ΕΥΦΡΟΣΥΝΟΣ   ὁ ΜΑΓΕΙΡΟΣ

HYMN TO ST EUPHROSYNOS THE COOK

TROPARION

*You lived in great humility,
in labors of ascetism
and in purity of soul.
O righteous Euphrosynos,
by a mystical vision you
demonstrated the heavenly
joy which you had found.
Therefore make us worthy
to be partakers of
your intercessions.*

HISTORICAL NOTE

Euphrosynos—pronounced *Ĕf-rō´-sē-nōs* and meaning 'cheery' or 'merry'—was the name of a legendary monk of the ninth century. More than one Mediterranean and Middle Eastern Christian church claim him as a native son and saint. As the story goes, Euphrosynos was an uncultured peasant boy who entered a monastery at a young age and worked as a kitchen helper, enduring the scorn of more learned and erudite monks. Due to his appearance in the dream of an elder monk, in which Euphrosynos delighted in the garden of Paradise, he began to receive adulation from his community. Wishing to remain inconspicuous and modest, he fled the monastery to a destination unknown. He remains a virtuous model of patience, perseverance, gratitude, humility, and joy.